OUTRAGEOUS ORIGAMI

Duy Nguyen

STERLING INNOVATION
An imprint of Sterling Publishing Co., Inc.

New York / London
www.sterlingpublishing.com

STERLING and the distinctive Sterling logo are registered trademarks of
Sterling Publishing Co., Inc.

2   4   6   8   10   9   7   5   3   1

Published by Sterling Publishing Co., Inc.
387 Park Avenue South, New York, NY 10016
This work has been abridged from *Super-Easy Origami*
© 2005 by Duy Nguyen
Distributed in Canada by Sterling Publishing
c/o Canadian Manda Group, 165 Dufferin Street
Toronto, Ontario, Canada M6K 3H6
Distributed in the United Kingdom by GMC Distribution Services
Castle Place, 166 High Street, Lewes, East Sussex, England BN7 1XU
Distributed in Australia by Capricorn Link (Australia) Pty. Ltd.
P.O. Box 704, Windsor, NSW 2756, Australia

Printed in China
Sterling ISBN-13: 978-1-4027-5618-4
ISBN-10: 1-4027-5618-6

For information about custom editions, special sales, premium and
corporate purchases, please contact Sterling Special Sales
Department at 800-805-5489 or specialsales@sterlingpublishing.com.

CONTENTS

INTRODUCTION

Have you ever seen someone take a simple square of paper and fold it into strange and wonderful shapes? Folding paper like that is called Origami, and you can do it, too. It will take some practice. But once you know your valley fold from your mountain fold and can follow a few other simple directions, you are on your way to making those strange and wonderful shapes on your own . . . as many as you like!

Here are step-by-step directions for making a puppy, a flower, a goldfish, a butterfly, and more. There's some colorful origami paper here, too. But don't take it out yet! You are sure to make a lot of folding mistakes while you are learning. So don't use the special origami paper for practice. Cut some large squares from sheets of plain white or colored paper to practice on (see page 47). Then, when you are ready, get out the bright-colored origami paper, and go to it!

ORIGAMI PAPER

Origami is folded using a special thin paper. It comes in all colors and in different size squares–usually 6 or 8 inches (about 15 or 20 centimeters). Here, we have supplied 50 6-inch sheets: 10 each of 5 different color patterns, specially printed for the projects in this book.

WHEN CHOOSING ORIGAMI PAPER:

1. Look for paper that folds well and doesn't tear easily.

2. If colored paper is too heavy or thick, the color might "break" at the fold.

3. Some papers stretch, so they are not good for doing origami.

4. Try out new paper by folding some scraps.

HOW TO FOLD ORIGAMI

All these projects begin with a square. Fold the paper one step at a time, following the instruction and the picture. As you make the fold for one step, look at the picture for the next step. That's what it should look like after you make the fold. As you fold the paper, make sure the edges of the paper line up. When you make folds at the corners, they should come to nice points. Do your origami on a clean, flat surface. Press down and run your finger, or a fingernail, down the length of the fold to press it in neatly.

FOLD LINES AND SYMBOLS

These fold lines and marks will guide you:

VALLEY FOLD LINE	MOUNTAIN FOLD LINE	CREASE LINE
– – – – – – – – – –	· · · · · · · · · · · · · ·	————————

CUT LINE (USE SCISSORS)	PLEAT FOLD	FOLD TO THE RIGHT–FOLLOW THE ARROW
⊥⊥⊥⊥⊥⊥⊥⊥⊥⊥⊥		

FOLD TO THE LEFT–FOLLOW THE ARROW	FOLD THEN UNFOLD–DOUBLE HEADED ARROW	ROTATE OR TURN THE FORM OVER

THE BASIC FOLDS
VALLEY FOLD

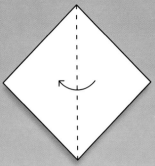

1. Fold the paper forward (toward you). Fold on the dashed line. Follow the arrow.

2. You've made a valley fold.

MOUNTAIN FOLD

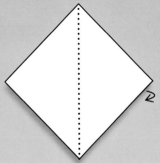

1. Fold the paper backward (away from you). Make the fold on the dotted line.

2. You've made a mountain fold.

TIP

To remember which line is valley and which is mountain, think of the line of dashes as a stream running down a valley, and the line of dots as the mountain peaks sticking up.

7

KITE FOLD

1. Valley fold a square of paper from corner to corner.

2. Unfold the paper to make a crease in the center.

3. Valley fold one side on the dashed line. Line up the paper against the center crease.

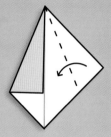 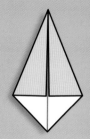

4. Valley fold the other side in, too.

5. This is a kite fold.

PRACTICE WITH THE KITE FOLD

 OR

1. Valley fold a kite form like this:
   Fold it toward you on the dashed line.

1. Mountain fold a kite form like this:
   Fold it away from you on the dotted line.

INSIDE REVERSE FOLD

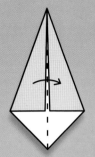

1. Start with a kite fold. Valley fold it in half on the dashed line.

2. Pull the top point to the right and make mountain folds front and back on the dotted line.

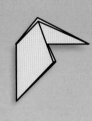

3. It's an inside reverse fold.

OUTSIDE REVERSE FOLD

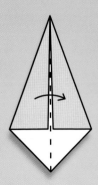

1. Start with a kite fold. Valley fold it in half on the dashed line.

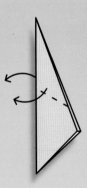

2. Pull the top point so it turns inside out. Make valley folds front and back on the dashed line.

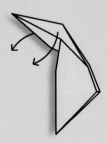

3. This is what it looks like while you are folding.

4. It's an outside reverse fold.

PLEAT FOLD

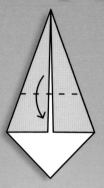

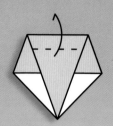

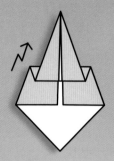

1. Start with a kite fold. Valley fold it on the dashed line.

2. Now valley fold back.

3. It's a pleat fold.

TIP

To make a clean fold, position the paper so that the fold line will lie exactly where you want it. Then, press with your thumb or finger-nail to make a nice smooth crease on the fold line.

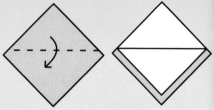

TIP

Make sure that edges line up and that tips come to a clean point when they are supposed to.

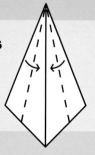

NOTE

All the projects in this book start with a regular square.

OUTRAGEOUS PROJECTS

FLOWER

Flowers come in many colors. You can make this one blue, yellow, or whatever you'd like.

1. Valley fold the square in half on the dashed line.

2. Valley fold the paper again on the dashed line, and unfold.

3. Valley fold and unfold again.

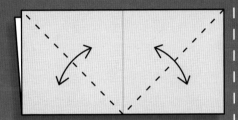

4. Using the creases, make inside reverse folds on both sides. The folds on both sides will be mountain folds.

5. Make inside reverse folds again.
(See the tip on page 16 for help with the inside reverse fold.)

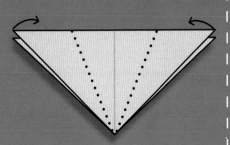

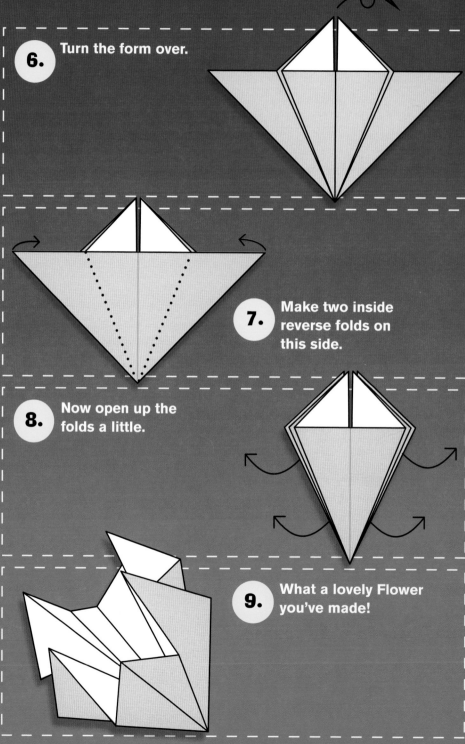

6. Turn the form over.

7. Make two inside reverse folds on this side.

8. Now open up the folds a little.

9. What a lovely Flower you've made!

PUPPY

It's so easy to make this adorable puppy.
You can make him a friend, too.

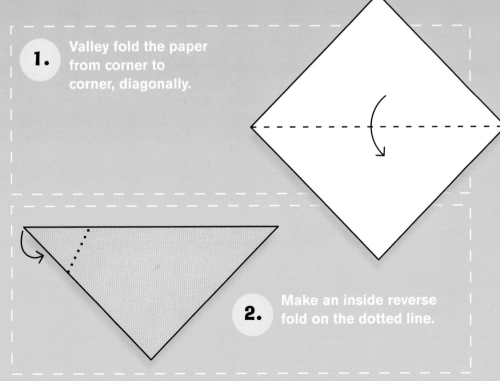

1. Valley fold the paper from corner to corner, diagonally.

2. Make an inside reverse fold on the dotted line.

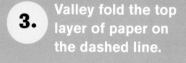

3. Valley fold the top layer of paper on the dashed line.

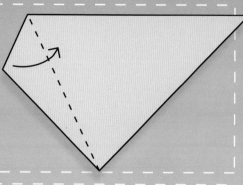

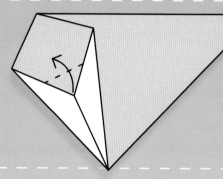

4. Make a valley fold upward on the dashed line.

TIP

Here's a way to make an inside or outside reverse fold easier to do. First, valley fold and then mountain fold the paper on the line and unfold it. Then, turn the creased folds on each side into mountain or valley folds. An inside reverse fold has mountain folds on both sides. An outside reverse fold has valley folds on both sides.

5. Valley fold the tip to make the puppy's nose.

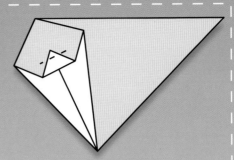

6. Valley fold the section on the right.

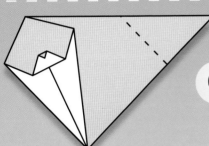

7. Turn the puppy to sit upright.

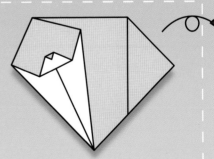

8. Here is the Puppy. Color nose and make eyes with markers.

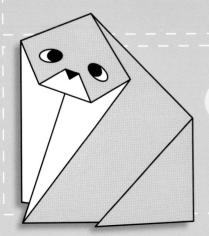

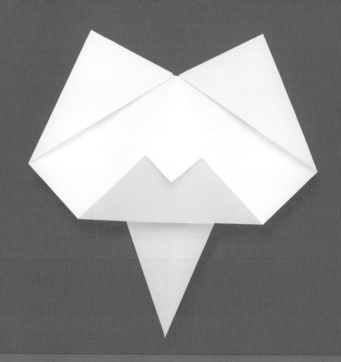

The cat is yellow, but you can make yours any color you wish.

1. Valley fold the square in half to crease, then unfold.

2. Valley fold the sides inward to the crease.

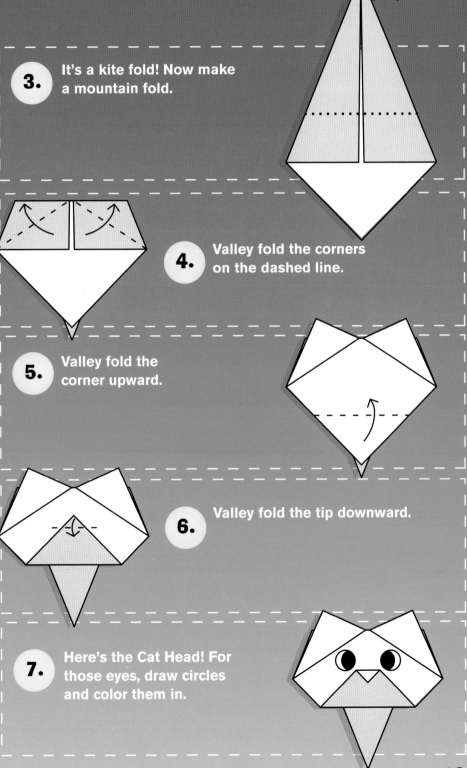

3. It's a kite fold! Now make a mountain fold.

4. Valley fold the corners on the dashed line.

5. Valley fold the corner upward.

6. Valley fold the tip downward.

7. Here's the Cat Head! For those eyes, draw circles and color them in.

BULL

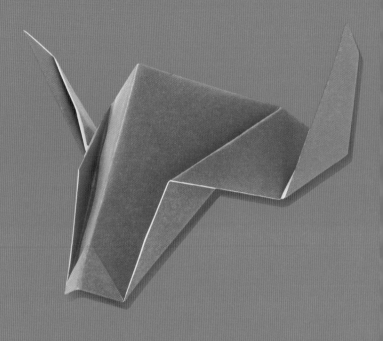

You don't need to be a matador to make this bull. Give it a shot!

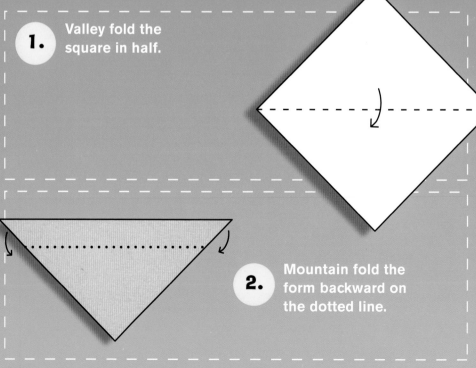

1. Valley fold the square in half.

2. Mountain fold the form backward on the dotted line.

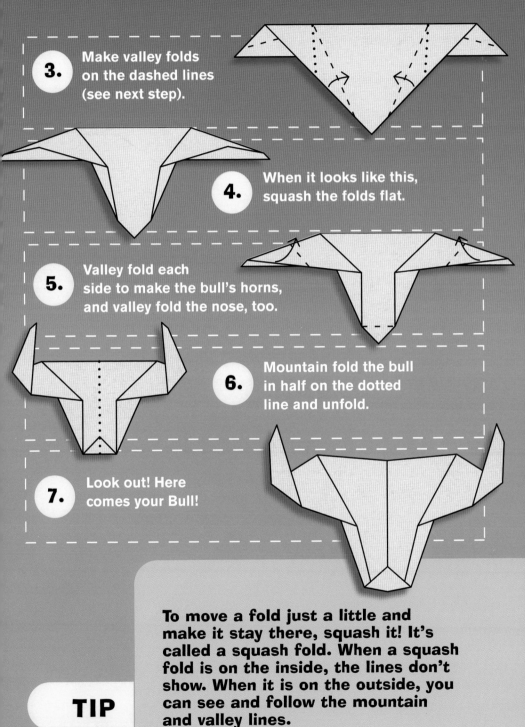

3. Make valley folds on the dashed lines (see next step).

4. When it looks like this, squash the folds flat.

5. Valley fold each side to make the bull's horns, and valley fold the nose, too.

6. Mountain fold the bull in half on the dotted line and unfold.

7. Look out! Here comes your Bull!

TIP

To move a fold just a little and make it stay there, squash it! It's called a squash fold. When a squash fold is on the inside, the lines don't show. When it is on the outside, you can see and follow the mountain and valley lines.

Don't make just one goldfish. Draw a fishbowl big enough to hold two or three.

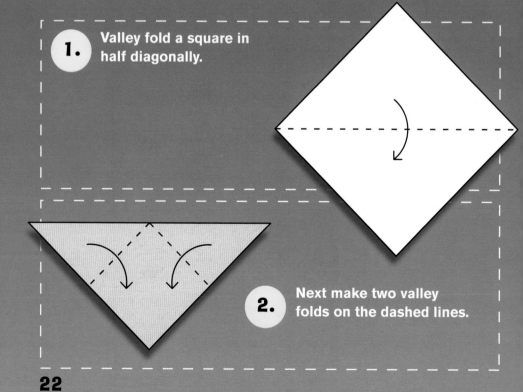

1. Valley fold a square in half diagonally.

2. Next make two valley folds on the dashed lines.

22

BUTTERFLY

It's fun to make lots of colorful butterflies.

1. Valley fold the square paper in half.

2. Valley fold to make a crease, then unfold.

3. Valley fold both layers upward together.

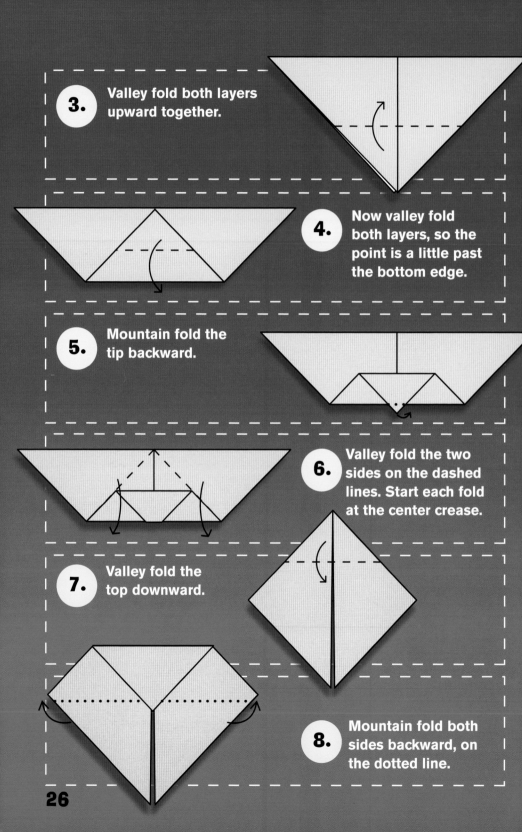

4. Now valley fold both layers, so the point is a little past the bottom edge.

5. Mountain fold the tip backward.

6. Valley fold the two sides on the dashed lines. Start each fold at the center crease.

7. Valley fold the top downward.

8. Mountain fold both sides backward, on the dotted line.

9. Turn the form over to work on the other side.

10. Pull the two sides outward a little (see next step) and squash fold (see the tip on page 21).

11. Valley fold the tips of the wings and the top point.

12. Valley fold in half, then unfold.

13. What a lovely Butterfly you've made!

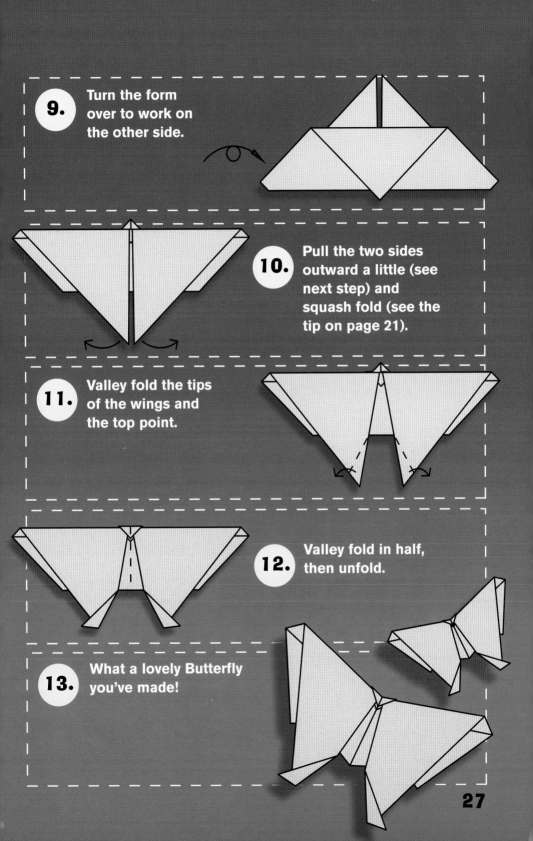

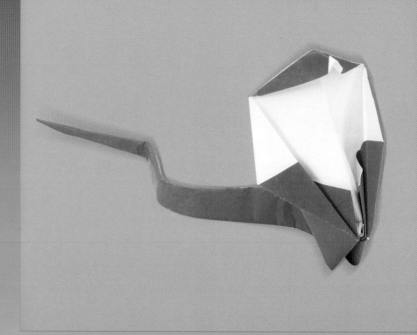

You don't have to worry about getting too close to this cobra.

TIP

Add color to your white paper with highlighter, crayon, or paint. Or set your computer's printer to print out solid or patterned color paper for use in origami. You can even make two-sided color paper for special projects, like this King Cobra!

1. Start with a square. Make a valley fold on the dashed line, then unfold it.

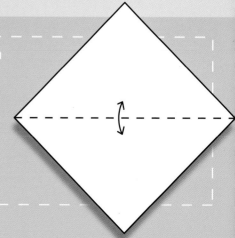

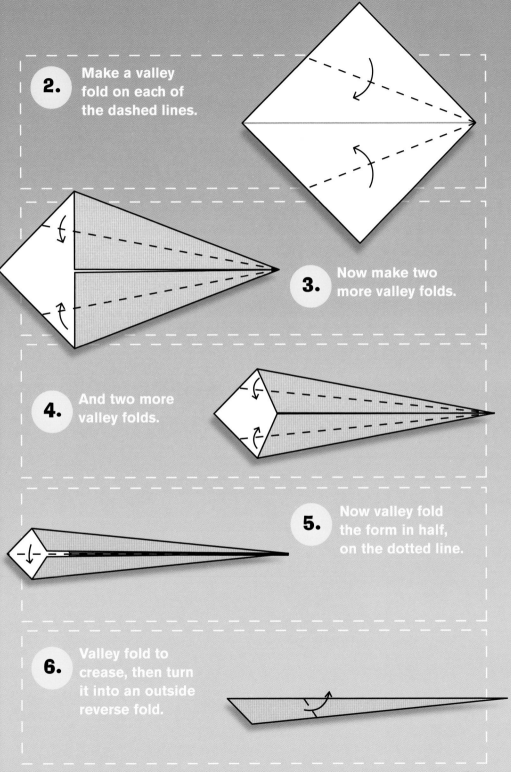

2. Make a valley fold on each of the dashed lines.

3. Now make two more valley folds.

4. And two more valley folds.

5. Now valley fold the form in half, on the dotted line.

6. Valley fold to crease, then turn it into an outside reverse fold.

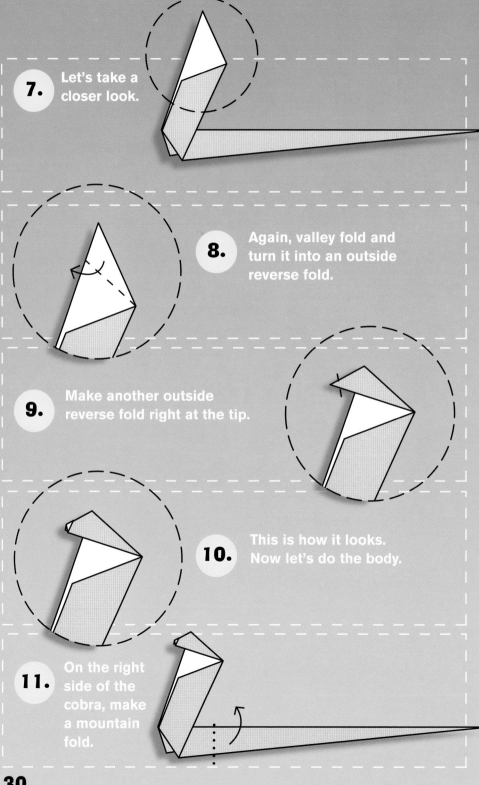

7. Let's take a closer look.

8. Again, valley fold and turn it into an outside reverse fold.

9. Make another outside reverse fold right at the tip.

10. This is how it looks. Now let's do the body.

11. On the right side of the cobra, make a mountain fold.

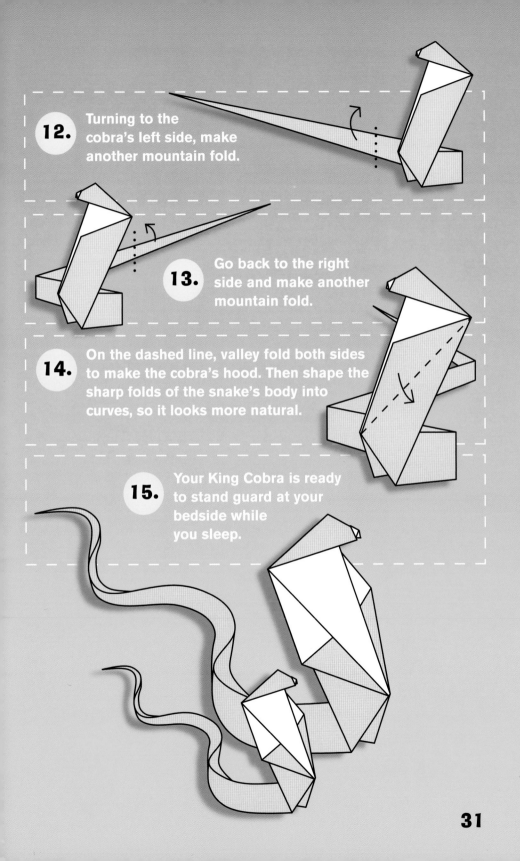

12. Turning to the cobra's left side, make another mountain fold.

13. Go back to the right side and make another mountain fold.

14. On the dashed line, valley fold both sides to make the cobra's hood. Then shape the sharp folds of the snake's body into curves, so it looks more natural.

15. Your King Cobra is ready to stand guard at your bedside while you sleep.

31

How would you like your own elephant?
Let's get started.

1. Valley fold on the dashed line, then unfold.

2. Make these two valley folds.

32

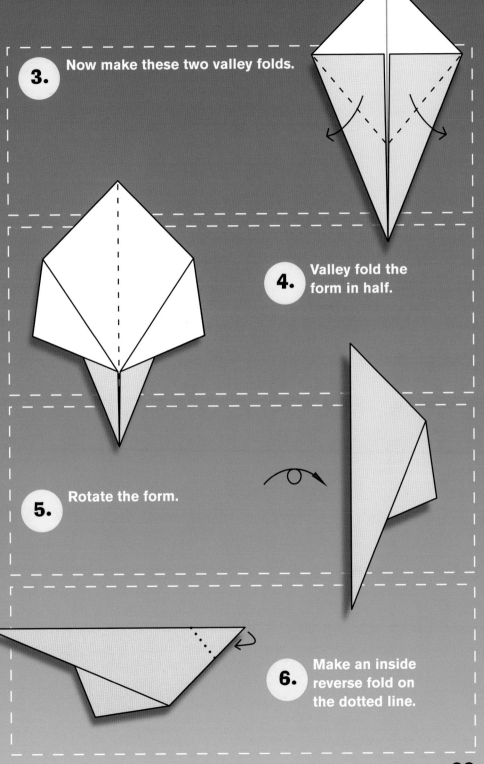

3. Now make these two valley folds.

4. Valley fold the form in half.

5. Rotate the form.

6. Make an inside reverse fold on the dotted line.

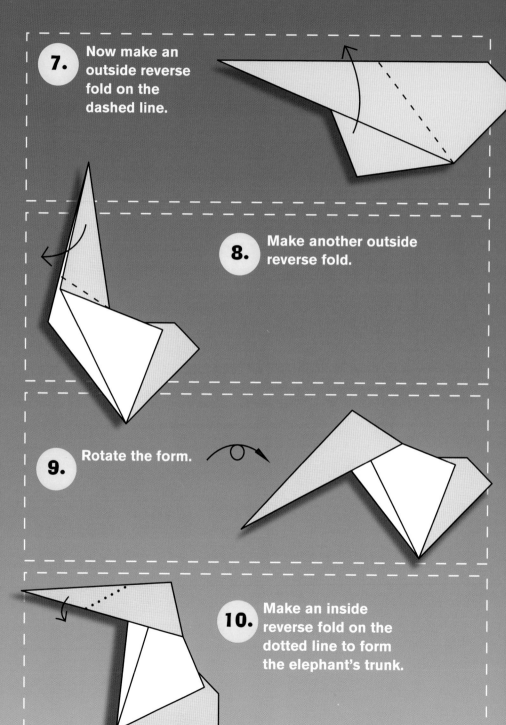

7. Now make an outside reverse fold on the dashed line.

8. Make another outside reverse fold.

9. Rotate the form.

10. Make an inside reverse fold on the dotted line to form the elephant's trunk.

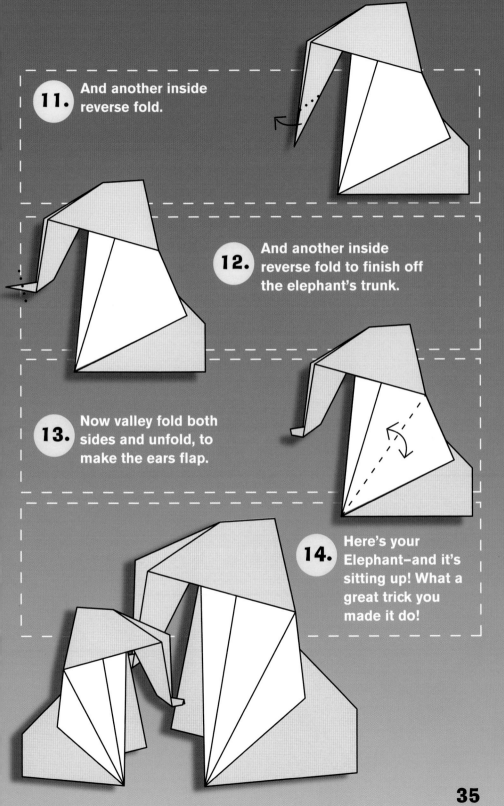

11. And another inside reverse fold.

12. And another inside reverse fold to finish off the elephant's trunk.

13. Now valley fold both sides and unfold, to make the ears flap.

14. Here's your Elephant—and it's sitting up! What a great trick you made it do!

This falcon may take quite a few steps, but you'll be creating a beautiful bird.

1. Valley fold a square diagonally.

2. Valley fold the top layer upward.

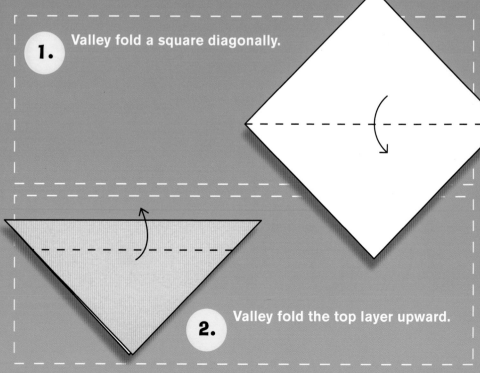

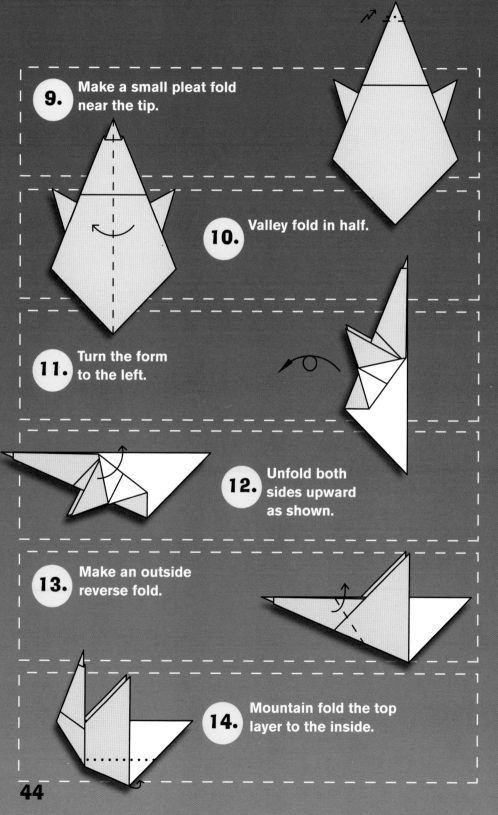

9. Make a small pleat fold near the tip.

10. Valley fold in half.

11. Turn the form to the left.

12. Unfold both sides upward as shown.

13. Make an outside reverse fold.

14. Mountain fold the top layer to the inside.

3. Does it look like this? Good! Now valley fold and unfold to crease.

4. Valley fold one side. Line the paper up against the crease.

5. Now make a valley fold on the dashed line.

6 Valley fold the left side, like you did before on the right.

7. And valley fold back again.

8. Turn the form over.

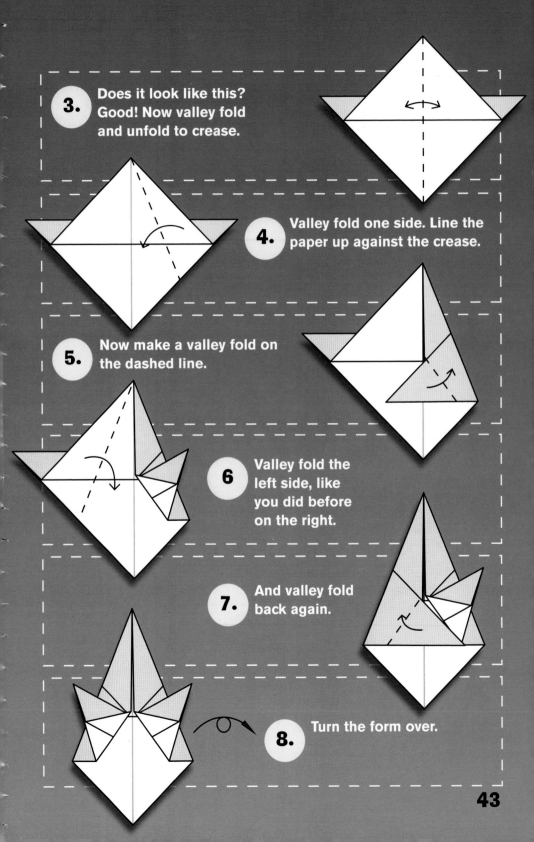

43

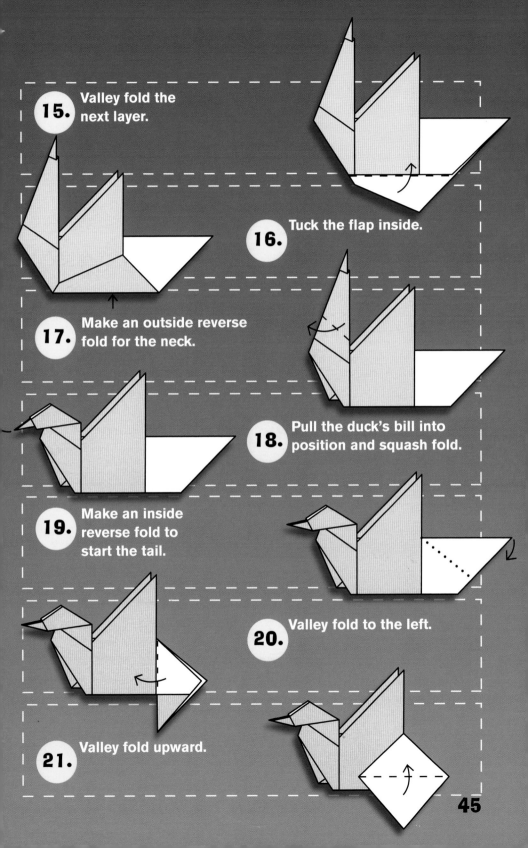

15. Valley fold the next layer.

16. Tuck the flap inside.

17. Make an outside reverse fold for the neck.

18. Pull the duck's bill into position and squash fold.

19. Make an inside reverse fold to start the tail.

20. Valley fold to the left.

21. Valley fold upward.

45

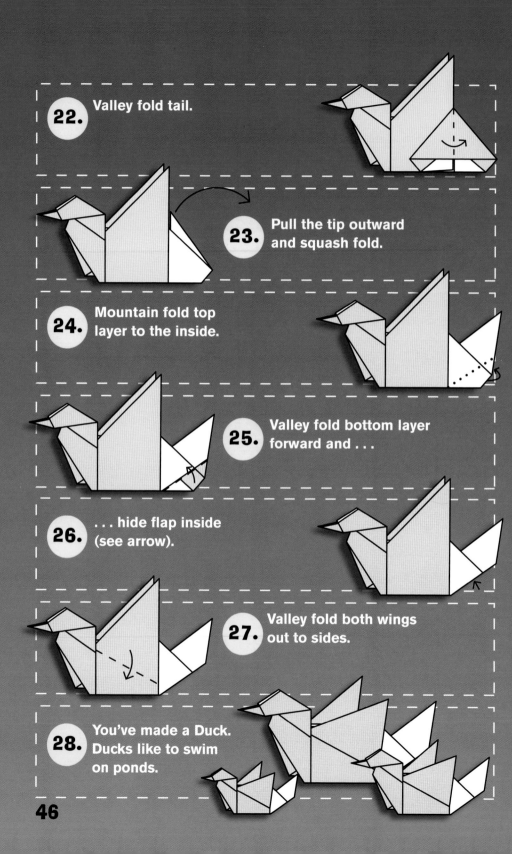

22. Valley fold tail.

23. Pull the tip outward and squash fold.

24. Mountain fold top layer to the inside.

25. Valley fold bottom layer forward and . . .

26. . . . hide flap inside (see arrow).

27. Valley fold both wings out to sides.

28. You've made a Duck. Ducks like to swim on ponds.

SQUARING-OFF PAPER

Here is an easy way to get
square paper for practice
and for folding projects.

1. Take any sheet of
paper. Valley fold it
diagonally to the
opposite edge.

2. Cut the edge of the
paper off as shown.

3. Unfold . . .

4. . . . and the paper is square!

INDEX